We Are Inseparable

BUILDING RELATIONSHIPS AND RESILIENCE WITH
OUR BWINDI MOUNTAIN GORILLA NEIGHBORS

LAURA SANDERS ARNDT

in collaboration with people living and working
around Uganda's Bwindi Impenetrable National Park

Copyright Information

© 2025 Global GreenSTEM.

Original © 2003. Registration Number / Date: TXu001081064 / 2003-05-08

Original title: The mountain gorillas and people surrounding the parks of East Central Africa.

ALL RIGHTS RESERVED. This book contains material protected under International and Federal Copyright Laws and Treaties. Any unauthorized reprint or use of this material is prohibited. No part of this book may be reproduced or transmitted in any form or by any means, electronic or mechanical, including photocopying, recording, or by any information storage and retrieval system, without express written permission from the author/publisher.

ISBN: 979-8-89079-249-5 (paperback)
ISBN: 979-8-89079-250-1 (ebook)

Title inspiration: "We are Inseparable"

"Batwa have historically shared the forest with mountain gorillas and other animals. We view them as an inseparable inherent part of humans."
- Batwa elder Geofrey BUCHEBE

Image Attributions

Photos are credited and/or attributed in the lower right corner of the card on which they appear. For a complete list of asset attributions, contact lauraarndt@globalgreenstem.com.

Cover Photos

Credit: Laura Arndt (youth in forest), Erik Arndt (gorilla)

Icons

"BWINDI Sign" by Erik Arndt

"Gorilla" by Fran Couto, licensed under CC BY 3.0

"jungle" by Eucalyp, licensed under CC BY 3.0

"job" by andika, licensed under CC BY 3.0

"team" by Ajik Sugeng, licensed under CC BY 3.0

Table of Contents

Honoring Collaborators viii
Praise for *We are Inseparable* ix
Foreword by Dr. Gladys Kalema-Zikusoka,
Wildlife Veterinarian, Conservationist and Author xi

1 Bwindi Impenetrable National Park

B-1	Why was Bwindi Impenetrable National Park (BINP) established? 2	
B-2	Why does Bwindi Impenetrable National Park (BINP) want to protect mountain gorillas? 3	
B-3	How was this ancient forest protected before becoming a national park? 4	
B-4	Why is the park called Bwindi Impenetrable Forest? 5	
B-5	What makes Bwindi Impenetrable National Park's diversity so unique? 6	
B-6	How have BINP and communities built mutually beneficial relationships? 7	
B-7	How does UWA's wildlife compensation program help community-BINP relationships? 8	
B-8	What's the relationship between the mountain gorillas and people living in neighboring communities? 9	
B-9	What's the relationship between the forest and people living in neighboring communities? 10	
B-10	What is the relationship between the Batwa and the forest? 11	
B-11	What is the relationship between the Batwa and the mountain gorillas? 12	
B-12	What happened to the Batwa when the BINP was formed? 13	

2 Mountain Gorillas

Physical Characteristics

G-1	Long Fur	18
G-2	No Tail	19
G-3	Thumbs on Hands & Feet	20
G-4	Long Arms, Broad Shoulders	21
G-5	Big Round Belly	22
G-6	Unique Nose Prints	23
G-7	Silver Fur on Adult Male	24
G-8	Teeth	25

Daily Activities

G-9	Daily Routine: Walk, Eat, Rest	28
G-10	Eat Plants	29
G-11	Rest & Play	30
G-12	Build Night Nests	31
G-13	Groom Each Other	32
G-14	Climb Trees	33
G-15	Get Curious	34
G-16	Lifespan of Gorillas	35

Communication

G-17	Belches	38
G-18	Hoots & Roars	39
G-19	Chest Beats	40
G-20	Face Expressions	41
G-21	Odors & Smells	42
G-22	Charges & Bluffs	43

Group Roles

G-23	Family Groups	46
G-24	Dominant Silverback Male	47
G-25	Blackback Males	48
G-26	Additional Silverbacks	49
G-27	Adult Females	50
G-28	Pregnant Females	51
G-29	Dads	52
G-30	Moms	53
G-31	Babies	54
G-32	Juveniles and Teenagers	55
G-33	Lone Gorillas	56

3 Ecosystems of Bwindi Impenetrable Forest

Forest Ecosystems

F-1	Land of Mist	60
F-2	Mountain Rainforest	61
F-3	Sunny Meadows	62
F-4	Thick Undergrowth	63
F-5	Forest Soil	64
F-6	Forest Water Catchment	65
F-7	Groundwater to Wells	66
F-8	Forest Streams	67

Animals of the Forest

F-9	Gorillas (Engagi)	70
F-10	Chimpanzees (Empundu)	71
F-11	Forest Elephants (Enjojo)	72
F-12	Duikers (Efumbiri)	73

F-13	Baboons (Enkobe)	74
F-14	Colobus Monkey (Enkyende)	75
F-15	Golden Monkey (Enkyende)	76
F-16	Red-Tailed Monkey (Enkyende)	77
F-17	L'Hoest's Monkey (Enkyende)	78
F-18	Bush Pig (Empunu)	79
F-19	Pangolin (Engamba)	80
F-20	Bees (Enjokyi)	81
F-21	Butterflies (Ekyihuguhugu)	82
F-22	Birds (Enyonyi)	83

Plants of the Forest

F-23	Mahogany Tree (Omuyovii)	86
F-24	Ficus Trees (Ekyitoma)	87
F-25	Ceiba Tree (Ekitoma)	88
F-26	African Tree Fern (Ekigunju)	89
F-27	Edible & Medicinal Plants	90
F-28	Favorite Plants of People	91
F-29	Food for Wildlife	92
F-30	Favorite Foods of Gorillas	93

4 Jobs supporting the forest and wildlife

J-1	Park & UWA Staff	96
J-2	Ranger Patrols	97
J-3	Ranger Guides & Trackers	98
J-4	Gorilla Guardians	99
J-5	Wildlife Vets & Scientists	100
J-6	Porters for Tourists	101
J-7	Drivers for Tourists	102
J-8	Lodging & Service Staff	103

J-9	Artists & Handcrafters.	104
J-10	Coffee Farmers	105
J-11	Conservation Org. Staff.	106

5 STEAM Conservation Projects

P-1	Reduce Human-Wildlife Conflict	110
P-2	Reduce Community Litter.	111
P-3	Repurpose Plastic Waste.	112
P-4	Reforest with Indigenous Trees	113
P-5	Grow Edible & Medicinal Plants.	114
P-6	Create Alternatives for Wood Fuel.	115
P-7	Improve Hygiene & Sanitation	116
P-8	Capture Rainwater	117
P-9	Clean Polluted Water	118
P-10	Provide a Reliable Protein Source	119
P-11	Educate with Art or App	120
P-12	Build Bee Apiaries	121

Learn About Bwindi Youth Guardians and STEAM Projects. 122

Bwindi Cards Story 124

About the Author 126

Honoring Collaborators
Webare Munonga

I am humbly grateful to the countless colleagues and friends from around the world who have, over decades, contributed your knowledge, photographs, time, and compassion to the different versions of the cards and now book. The content of the book began as interactive educational cards in 2001 with essential edits by Ugandan teachers, international scientists, and UWA park rangers. This most recent version, in both book and card format, has been a combined effort of the people I highlight here!

Dr. Gladys Kalema-Zikusoka, CEO of Conservation through Public Health (CTPH), and author of *Walking with Gorillas: Tales of an African Wildlife Vet*. Her integrated community-environment systems approach is a perfect match for my Global GreenSTEM solutions-based STEAM conservation projects. Together we established Bwindi Youth Guardian groups who are learning with these Bwindi Cards.

Staff of CTPH: Stephen Rubanga, Lawrence Zikusoka, Ebenezer Paul, Richard Bagyenyi, Kaamu Bukenya, Kanie Kaniwabo Elizabeth, Lilian Nandudu, Mary Leakey, Ssali Ogwals.

Gracious Twebaze, the CTPH: community coordinator who masterfully guides the Bwindi Youth Guardian (BYG) leaders and youth.

Mentors for the BYG groups: Ezera Mugyenyi, Sam Rugaba, David Matsiko, Safari Joseph, Patience Tushabomwe.

Batwa of Bwindi (Indigenous Knowledge Keepers of the Forest): Ezera Mugyenyi, with 85-year-old Batwa elder Geofrey Buchebe, and Marthias Ngabirano.

Our first **Bwindi Youth Guardians and leaders** in Mukono and Bujengwe Parishes. Your STEAM conservation projects are showing your villages and the world how young people can design and do projects with sustainable solutions to systemic conservation problems.

Erik Nshuti Arndt, my thought partner and editor, and the designer and builder of these beautiful cards.

Praise for *We are Inseparable*

I recommend *We Are Inseparable* for anyone committed to the future of mountain gorillas and wishing to engage in long term efforts to ensure they live in harmony with human beings in protected areas, supported by local communities. This book will become a valued resource for anyone interested in these issues, whether field staff working for national parks, conservation non-profit organisations, local community organisations, school children, staff at lodges, tour operators, and committed guests visiting the area who wish to be engaged in safeguarding the future of gorillas. The book is written as a field guide to easily find answers to questions about the gorillas and the forest habitats, the vital connection to communities, about conservation jobs and projects being done in the area. Its wide-ranging coverage will be of enormous benefit as an education resource, especially in local communities. The simplicity, graphics, and clear organization make it easy to use.

I have known Laura since 2001 when Volcanoes Safaris' first driver guide in Rwanda looked after Laura on her visits to Volcanoes and Bwindi National Parks and local schools. He got to use the prototype version of these cards.
*Praveen Moman, Founder of Volcanoes Safaris

Through these cards [now a book] children know why they should conserve, which will influence the future. Great appreciation as cards have planted a positive attitude to the young generation to conserve wildlife in BINP.
*David Matsiko, founder and director of Rugando Parents School, Uganda. Bwindi Youth Guardian leader and mentor

We worked closely with Laura to make sure the book includes accurate stories about the ancient Indigenous Batwa and our relationship with the forest, gorillas, chimpanzees, and other wildlife. We are the Keepers of Forest even though we are no longer able to live in our forest home. As the oldest Bantu tribes of the Great lakes region, we were happily living in harmony in the Bwindi Forest for 70,000 years. We hope the book will bring accurate information about the Batwa and about the forest to the minds and thoughts of readers.
*Ezera MUGYENYI, Batwa, founder of Bwindi Batwa Culture Rocks & Cave Association, Bwindi Youth Guardian mentor

(Translated into Rukiga) Turikukora na Laura Arndt owizire ahabwa CTPH/ NGS turikugyezeho okuhandika ekitabo kugira Ngu abantu abarikunkunda Kushoma, bamanye-ngu emigane ne nitekateko bya batwa ababeire barikutura omwihamba kubabire barikutura gye nengagi emyaka myingy emwireho 70,000 tukaturagye nengagi. Konka ahabwe abantu bingyi ahabwo kukunda ebyobuhangwa nengagi , hariho emiringo etaryemwe nemwe okubabasize kutuyamba nabantu boona abarikutura ehihi nehamba rya Bwindi.
*Ezera MUGYENYI, Batwa

Over the past 8 years working with Gorilla Habitat I have learned so much from the villagers, the international NGOs and the gorillas. For travelers trekking the mountain gorillas the book will provide you with an excellent overview of what you will experience and educate you on the complexity of the community.
*Stan Miller, founder of Gorilla Habitat organization

The book is truly marvelous. It MUST be published. The photographs are unique. They reveal the country, the people, gorillas, and forests as nothing else has done in the 53 years I have lived here! [About first card version, 2002]
*Rosamond (Roz) Halsey Carr, friend of mountain gorilla researcher Dian Fossey, author of Land of a Thousand Hills

I've spent years taking people on gorillas tracking tours, and learned a lot from these cards (first version in 2002). It is a must for whoever wishes to know all about the gorillas. It will help them understand that the gorillas are in the same business as us: raising, protecting, and feeding their families with care and love without any intent to interfere or harm the people.
*Itangayenda (Itanga) Viateur, Tour Guide for Volcano Safaris

The cards [first version, 2002] are viewed with pure excitement and anticipation as the children learn about the mountain gorillas, the forests of the national parks, the benefits and concerns about living together and the solutions to live in harmony. The children are [now] aware of the conservation concerns of this endangered species and the importance of finding solutions to help the animals and people surrounding the park.
*Zachary Dusingizimana and Chrissie Abel, teachers at Rosamond Carr's Imabazi Orphanage in Rwanda

Foreword
by Dr. Gladys Kalema-Zikusoka,
Wildlife Veterinarian, Conservationist and Author

At Conservation Through Public Health (CTPH), we believe that the well-being of both wildlife and people are deeply intertwined, and nowhere is this connection more evident than at Bwindi Impenetrable National Park. Mountain gorillas are threatened by disease from closely genetically related humans, loss of habitat and injuries from snares and spears through poaching for other wild animals including duikers and bush pigs as well as climate change. The Bwindi Cards are a crucial tool in advancing our shared mission of protecting the mountain gorillas and the forest ecosystem while uplifting the communities living around the park. These cards represent not only knowledge about protecting gorillas and other wildlife, but also the bond we share with the natural world—a bond that is, as the Batwa elder Geofrey so eloquently put it, inseparable.

The Bwindi Cards are more than educational materials; they are a bridge between generations, places, and species. Through them, the youth of Bwindi, especially the Bwindi Youth Guardians (BYG) can learn about the delicate balance of the forest ecosystem, conservation careers, and great examples of innovative STEAM (Science, Technology, Engineering, Art and Math) projects that are vital for preserving our heritage. Each card highlights important information about the gorillas and other wildlife, the local communities, and their stories, as well as the incredible natural wonders of Bwindi. From the rangers who safeguard the park to the community members who contribute to gorilla conservation and tourism, the cards reflect the unity of purpose that drives us all.

When I was first introduced to these cards, I immediately appreciated how much they can educate the rangers when guiding visitors to the gorillas to broaden their knowledge of this incredible national park, the wildlife it protects, and the roles they play within it. By providing a digital version, we hope to equip rangers with an invaluable resource that not only enhances their expertise but also allows them to share their passion and knowledge with tourists. Imagine the profound impact of turning a gorilla trek or a forest walk into an interpretive experience, where visitors leave not just with memories but with a deeper understanding of the forest and its inhabitants.

Over the past three decades I have been inspired by the increasing desire of local communities to want to protect the Gorillas and other wildlife as they come to the realization that our health and wellbeing is interdependent. We are inseparable—from each other, from the wildlife, and from the land. This is the heart of CTPH's mission, and it is the hope we carry forward with every set of Bwindi Cards. Together, we can ensure that future generations inherit not only the knowledge of conservation, but also the commitment to living in harmony with the forest and its remarkable species.

I would like to congratulate Laura Arndt and Global Green STEM, for this wonderful initiative. And hope that it will contribute significantly to the goals of Uganda Wildlife Authority and stakeholders - conserving for current and future generations.

— Dr. Gladys Kalema-Zikusoka
Founder and CEO, Conservation Through Public Health (CTPH)

We Are Inseparable

1

Bwindi Impenetrable National Park

B-1   Why was Bwindi Impenetrable National Park (BINP) established?
B-2   Why does Bwindi Impenetrable National Park (BINP) want to protect mountain gorillas?
B-3   How was this ancient forest protected before becoming a national park?
B-4   Why is the park called Bwindi Impenetrable Forest?
B-5   What makes Bwindi Impenetrable National Park's diversity so unique?
B-6   How have BINP and communities built mutually beneficial relationships?
B-7   How does UWA's wildlife compensation program help community-BINP relationships?
B-8   What's the relationship between the mountain gorillas and people living in neighboring communities?
B-9   What's the relationship between the forest and people in living in neighboring communities?
B-10 What is the relationship between the Batwa and the forest?
B-11 What is the relationship between the Batwa and the mountain gorillas?
B-12 What happened to the Batwa when the BINP was formed?

Bwindi Impenetrable National Park

Park Establishment

Why was Bwindi Impenetrable National Park (BINP) established?

Bwindi Impenetrable National Park (BINP) was created in 1991 to protect the endangered mountain gorillas and their forest habitat. By designating the land as a national park, people could no longer go into the forest to cut trees, convert pieces of forest into farmland, gather plants, harvest animals for protein food, or poach gorillas or other animals. The park has built relationships with nearby communities, providing ways for them to benefit from the park in sustainable ways.

Bwindi Impenetrable National Park

Protecting Gorillas

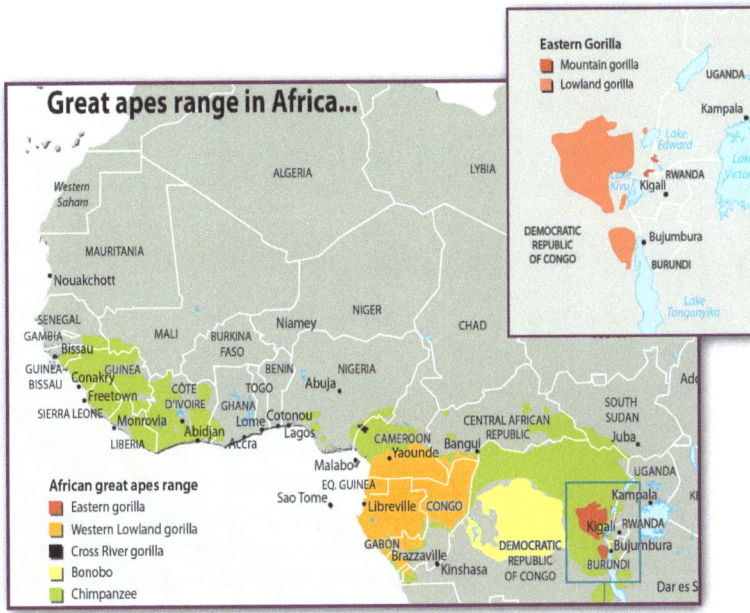

Why does Bwindi Impenetrable National Park (BINP) want to protect mountain gorillas?

Mountain gorillas are an endangered species protected by international law. As of the 2018 census only 1,063 mountain gorillas remain in the world, with over 450 in Bwindi. Outside of Bwindi-Mgahina Conservation Area, mountain gorillas can only be found in one other place: the Virunga Mountains shared by the Democratic Republic of Congo and Rwanda. Because their forest habitat is now a national park, it is illegal for people to disturb their forest habitat. People cannot capture or kill these gorillas.

We Are Inseparable *Photos: Riccardo Pravettoni*

Bwindi Impenetrable National Park B-3

History of Protection

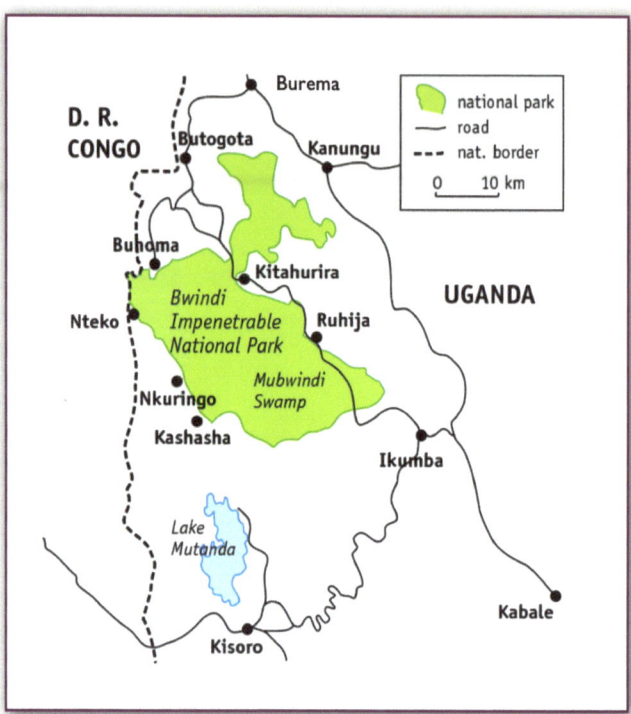

How was this ancient forest protected before becoming a national park?

This area was first protected from development in 1932 when two pieces of forest were designated Crown Forest Reserves. In 1942 the area became Bwindi Impenetrable Forest Reserve. In 1964 the reserve was given additional protection for its mountain gorillas by becoming an animal sanctuary and was renamed the Impenetrable Central Forest Reserve. In 1991, Bwindi Impenetrable Forest was gazetted as a national park, and a few years later as a UNESCO World Heritage Site in 1994.

Bwindi Impenetrable National Park B-4

Meaning of *Bwindi*

Why is the park called Bwindi Impenetrable Forest?

The story of how Bwindi got its name comes from the Indigenous Batwa. A family was migrating through the forest long ago. When they could not get around a large swamp, the spirits of the swamp said they would help if the family sacrificed their daughter Nnyinamukari. After much thought, the family finally honored the spirits' request and threw the girl into the water to drown. They were then able to cross safely to the other side. When others heard the story, they began calling the forest and swamp Mubwindi Bwa Nynamuraki, meaning "muddy, swampy place full of darkness." Nyinamukari is the name for "maiden." Ever since then, communities around the forest have called the forest Bwindi and the swamp Mubwindi. When the forest became a national park, Bwindi was kept as the official name.

Bwindi Impenetrable National Park   B-5

Bwindi's Unique Diversity

What makes Bwindi Impenetrable National Park's diversity so unique?

Bwindi, over 25,000 years old, is one of the last ancient, old-growth forests. It is the source of five major rivers that flow across its steep ridges and valleys into Lake Edward. Bwindi has incredible biodiversity, with more than 1,000 flowering plants, more than 170 species of trees, and over 120 species of ferns. These diverse plants create a home for 120 species of mammals including the great ape chimpanzees and mountain gorillas, 350 species of birds, 200 species of butterflies, and 27 species of amphibians. Some of these animals, including 23 birds, 42 butterflies, and 11 amphibians, are endemic and are found nowhere else on Earth. While mountain gorillas aren't endemic, they live in only one other place on earth: the Virunga Mountains south of Bwindi where the borders of Uganda, Rwanda and the Democratic Republic of Congo meet. To protect the unique diversity of Bwindi, the park was designated a UNESCO Heritage Site in 1994.

We Are Inseparable   *Photo: Thomas Fuhrmann*

 *Bwindi Impenetrable National Park* B-6

Communities Near the Park

How have BINP and communities built mutually beneficial relationships?

Tourists from around the world travel to Bwindi to visit the national park and mountain gorillas, creating both pride and economic benefits for local communities. A portion of the entrance fees and gorilla trekking permit fees within BINP are given to nearby villages to use for building health centers, markets, schools and other community infrastructure and services. This means some mothers no longer have to travel many kilometers to deliver their babies. The park revenue sharing makes health education and support for family planning and other health issues accessible to more people. Local residents are able to get jobs as rangers and porters, and are able to set up ecotourism businesses that provide meals, lodging, and locally-made souvenirs for tourists.

Bwindi Impenetrable National Park   B-7

Wildlife Damage Compensation

How does UWA's wildlife compensation program help community-BINP relationships?

Wildlife, including gorillas and forest elephants, can freely move back and forth between the protected park's forest and the surrounding land that is filled with people's homes, crops, and livestock. Uganda Wildlife Authority has created a Wildlife Compensation Scheme to address any harm by wildlife to people, livestock, or property. This strengthens respectful relationships between the park, community, and wildlife. To initiate the process, the incident must be reported to UWA, police, or local council within 72 hours (3 days).

Bwindi Impenetrable National Park

Gorillas & Local Communities

What's the relationship between the mountain gorillas and people living in neighboring communities?

People feel both pride and respect for their mountain gorilla neighbors. These endangered animals are the reason tourists travel from around the world and pay park fees to go on a ranger-guided gorilla trek. When tourists stay in local communities and pay park fees, they are helping support the local economy and protect the forest. Most local residents only see gorillas if the animals wander out of the national park into neighboring fields and villages. They also need to pay park fees to go on ranger-guided gorilla treks in the forest. Most cannot afford this. When more opportunities are created for local adults and older youth to visit and learn about gorillas in their forest habitat, community commitment to care about and protect these animals and their forest home will grow.

We Are Inseparable   *Photo credit: Erik Arndt, Laura Arndt*

Bwindi Impenetrable National Park B-9

Forest & Local Communities

What's the relationship between the forest and people living in neighboring communities?

People living next to the national park recognize that human health and wellbeing are connected to the health of the forest and wildlife. The forest is a water catchment for community water supplies and helps stabilize the climate. Protecting the boundaries of the forest from deforestation reduces human-wildlife conflict. People can go into designated multi-use zones of the forest with park rangers to gather plants for weaving and handcrafts, food, and medicine. When local residents of all ages can take ranger-guided forest walks and learn about the wonders of this ancient forest, their pride and protective commitment increases because they understand more about the relationship between people, the forest, and wildlife.

Bwindi Impenetrable National Park B-10

Batwa & the Forest

What is the relationship between the Batwa and the forest?

"Batwa feel strongly attached and part of the fauna of the forest and the entire environment of Bwindi." - Batwa elder Geofrey BUCHEBE

This ancient forest is the traditional homeland of the Batwa, who have lived here for 80,000 years and are one of the oldest surviving Indigenous tribes in Africa. Like Indigenous communities across the world, they were an integral part of the forest ecosystem, coming to be known as "The Keepers of the Forest." When the park was formed, the Batwa were forcibly removed and now live in small communities on the edges of the forest. Their vast knowledge of the forest's plants, animals, and ecosystems has been built over millennia and is still passed from generation to generation in oral traditions. However, without access to their homelands, this knowledge is at risk of being lost.

Bwindi Impenetrable National Park B-11

Batwa & the Gorillas

Geofrey KANYAMUGARA
Batwa elder

What is the relationship between the Batwa and the mountain gorillas?

"Batwa have historically shared the forest with mountain gorillas and other animals. We view them as an inseparable inherent part of humans." - Batwa elder Geofrey BUCHEBE

As the quote suggests, the Batwa view mountain gorillas and other animals as their relatives. They learned from them and knew how to avoid conflicts with their much larger kin, deferring to gorillas when traveling through the forest. Killing or eating a mountain gorilla is completely taboo for the Batwa; to do so would be almost considered cannibalism.

Bwindi Impenetrable National Park B-12

Batwa Today

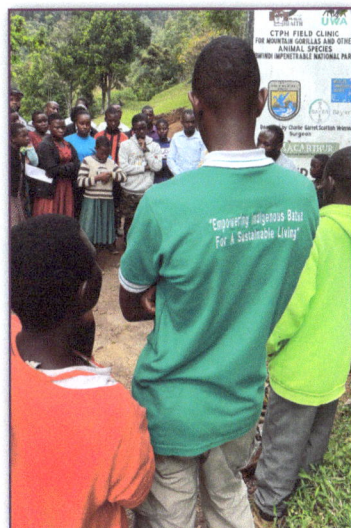

What happened to the Batwa when the BINP was formed?

The Batwa were evicted from their forest home when the park was formed in 1991. The government did not compensate them for their loss or give them new land, making them "conservation refugees." Much of their culture, traditions, knowledge, and wealth were lost when they were forced to give up their nomadic hunter-gatherer ways in the forest and become stationary agriculturalists.

Today, Batwa communities can be found on the edges of the forest, living as close as allowed to their original home. The communities are working to reduce severe poverty, malnutrition and other health problems, and discrimination in the village where they now live. Tourists are invited to visit to learn about Batwa knowledge and ways, and to support their emerging economic independence.

We Are Inseparable *Photos: Laura Arndt*

2

Mountain Gorillas

Physical Characteristics

Daily Activities

Communication

Group Roles

Physical Characteristics

(These physical adaptations help mountain gorillas survive and thrive in the forest.)

What does a mountain gorilla look like?

G-1 Long fur
G-2 No tail
G-3 Thumbs on hands and feet
G-4 Long arms, broad shoulders
G-5 Big round belly
G-6 Unique nose prints
G-7 Silver fur on adult male
G-8 Teeth

Physical Characteristics G-1

Long Fur

What does a mountain gorilla look like?

The long fur of mountain gorillas keeps them warm and dry in the cool temperatures and frequent rains. During a rainstorm gorillas might sit quietly, letting the water roll off their thick fur.

We Are Inseparable Photo: Ryoma Otsuka

Physical Characteristics G-2

No Tail

What does a mountain gorilla look like?

Monkeys have tails while the great apes – gorillas, chimps, bonobos, orangutans, and humans – do not. Monkeys use their tails to help balance as they move through trees. Scientists theorize that great apes lost their tail as they evolved to spend more time walking on two legs on the ground.

Physical Characteristics G-3

Thumbs on Hands & Feet

What does a mountain gorilla look like?

Mountain gorillas have opposable thumbs on their hands and feet. Just like people, their thumbs allow them to pick up small items and perform other precise actions that are impossible for other animals.

Physical Characteristics

Long Arms, Broad Shoulders

What does a mountain gorilla look like?

Mountain gorillas' massive shoulders and long arms give them incredible strength to pull down branches, pull up plant roots for food, lift and break heavy objects, and climb trees. A silverback's arm length from shoulder to fingertip can be 100 cm. His arm span, including both arms and his broad shoulders, can reach over three meters (300 cm)!

Physical Characteristics — G-5

Big Round Belly

What does a mountain gorilla look like?

A healthy mountain gorilla has a big round belly. Food sits in their stomach and intestines for a long time while it is being broken down, sending as many nutrients as possible into the blood vessels. This digestive process creates a lot of gas that gorillas noisily pass out of their bodies.

Physical Characteristics

Unique Nose Prints

G-6

What does a mountain gorilla look like?

Who's who? Each mountain gorilla has a different pattern of wrinkles on its nose that makes it unique, just like the fingerprints of people. Park staff and scientists use a gorilla's unique nose print to identify individuals.

Physical Characteristics

G-7

Silver Fur on Adult Male

What does a mountain gorilla look like?

An adult male mountain gorilla is called a "silverback." Between 12-15 years old, the black fur on his back grows in as silver, letting other gorillas know that he is sexually mature. A silverback's head is larger and more elongated that the other gorillas. He has a notable crest over his eyes and a prominent crest at the top of his head. This extended skull is where the muscles for his powerful jaw are attached. A silverback can weigh up to 180 kg (400 lbs) and is twice as large as a female.

Physical Characteristics

G-8

Teeth

What does a mountain gorilla look like?

Gorillas are plant eaters. They use their large pointed canine teeth to break apart tough plants like bark and twigs. Gorillas will show off their teeth when they feel threatened by intruders, need to protect their family, and want to show other males that they are stronger and dominant. The black stains on some gorillas' teeth are caused by the high amount of tannins in plants they eat. Coffee also has tannins, which is why people who drink coffee can get stained teeth over time.

Daily Activities

(These behavior adaptations help mountain gorillas survive and thrive in the forest.)

How do mountain gorillas spend their days?

G-9   Daily routine: Walk, eat, rest
G-10   Eat plants
G-11   Rest and play
G-12   Build night nests
G-13   Groom each other
G-14   Climb trees
G-15   Get curious
G-16   Life span of gorillas

Daily Activities

Daily Routine: Walk, Eat, Rest

How do mountain gorillas spend their days?

Walk, eat, rest, eat some more – the mountain gorillas' slow and quiet routine. About 30% of their day is spent eating, 30% moving through the forest to other eating spots, and 40% resting and sleeping. At sunrise the family members wake up, leave their night nests, and follow the silverback on a walk-and-eat morning. By mid-day it's time for a 2–3-hour nap, with other shorter rest breaks during the morning and afternoon. Young gorillas often fill this rest time with enthusiastic play. At sunset the gorillas build and sleep in night nests.

Daily Activities G-10

Eat Plants

How do mountain gorillas spend their days?

Mountain gorillas spend around 7 hours (30%) of the day eating leaves, stems, roots, and fruits of over 100 different plants. Their forest home is like a giant salad bowl. These plants also give gorillas most of the water they need. Bwindi gorillas also drink from streams. The family group's movement through the forest is affected by the amount, type, and location of plant foods as well as the location of other gorilla groups.

Daily Activities G-11

Rest & Play

How do mountain gorillas spend their days?

If mountain gorillas aren't eating, they are usually resting. Digesting plants takes a long time. This quiet time lets their bodies focus on breaking down the plant food so the nutrients can be absorbed into blood vessels. Rest time can also be a noisy time as gas from digestion passes out of their bodies.

Daily Activities G-12

Build Night Nests

How do mountain gorillas spend their days?

Mountain gorillas make new nests each night and for midday naps as they move around the forest. The nests are built on the ground or up in the trees by folding down flexible leafy stems to create soft pillows. Each adult gorilla makes a separate nest. Gorillas younger than 4 years old share a nest with their mother. They cluster their nests around the dominant silverback, the protector of the group.

Daily Activities G-13

Groom Each Other

How do mountain gorillas spend their days?

Rest time means grooming time. This common activity of mountain gorillas helps to keep their fur clean. Family members sit together to gently pick out dirt, tangles, plants, or bugs from another gorilla or from their own fur. Grooming is also calming and strengthens their relationships when one gorilla grooms another.

We Are Inseparable Photo: Nick Penny / CTPH

Daily Activities

G-14

Climb Trees

How do mountain gorillas spend their days?

Mountain gorillas are excellent climbers. In Bwindi, they are often seen feeding and sleeping in trees. Their long, strong arms help them to live and move as easily in trees as they do on the ground.

Daily Activities G-15

Get Curious

How do mountain gorillas spend their days?

Mountain gorillas are very curious! Habituated gorillas have learned that they are safe around some humans and will allow rangers, scientists, and tourists to sit nearby. Gorillas watch people, just as people watch gorillas. In rare instances, gorillas have looked at their reflections in camera lenses and examined people's belongings. This close contact because of curiosity can be harmful to gorillas, as some germs are easily passed to them from people and their belongings. For this reason, Uganda Wildlife Authority requires people to keep at least ten meters (11 yards or 33 feet) from gorillas even when the animals are roaming outside of the forest. On gorilla treks, it is critical that people closely follow the ranger's instructions to maintain a safe distance from the gorillas, to correctly wear a mask over nose and mouth, and to stay quiet and calm. Doing this will allow the gorillas to continue their natural behaviors safely.

Daily Activities

G-16

Lifespan of Gorillas

How do mountain gorillas spend their days?

Mountain gorillas can live for 45-50 years in their natural forest habitat. Silverback Ruhondeeza lived for 60 years. Bwindi gorillas are no longer dying from poaching. Common causes of illness and death are infections transferred during close contact with humans, human waste, human belongings, and livestock. Some life-threatening illnesses include respiratory infections and pneumonia. Park rangers and scientists are constantly monitoring gorilla health, identifying and treating illnesses or injuries connected to people and livestock. Scientists are often able to track the source of a gorilla's illness to specific communities, people, and livestock so that they, too, can receive medical treatment.

Communication

How do mountain gorillas communicate with each other, other wildlife, and people?

G-17 Belch
G-18 Hoots and roars
G-19 Chest beats
G-20 Face expressions
G-21 Odors and smells
G-22 Charges and bluffs

Communication — G-17

Belches

How do mountain gorillas communicate with each other, other wildlife, and people?

Mountain gorillas communicate using at least 22 different sounds. Tracker rangers and scientists understand the meanings of many, allowing them to understand and communicate with the gorillas.

The most common sound is called a belch. The soft throat-clearing "um-hmmm" is made between members of a group to say that all is well: "I'm ok. Are you ok?".

Communication

Hoots & Roars

How do mountain gorillas communicate with each other, other wildlife, and people?

Hoots are a series of hoo sounds that start quietly and get louder and louder. These sounds are sometimes followed by chest beating. Hoots are used to communicate with another mountain gorilla group or with a lone silverback. The sound can carry nearly a kilometer!

Roars are made by mountain gorilla males to scare away someone that makes them feel threatened. This could be a silverback threatening another male, or a male who is surprised or threatened by people or other animals.

Communication G-19

Chest Beats

How do mountain gorillas communicate with each other, other wildlife, and people?

One way a mountain gorilla communicates with others is by beating its fists on its chest. If a silverback wants a loud chest beat to get someone's attention, he will take several deep breaths to fill chest air sacs. This makes his chest into a big drum, sending the pok-pok sound of the chest beat miles away. This message might mean, "I do not like what you are doing" or "Look at me!" Silverbacks also beat their chests when they meet another gorilla group and may continue until one group leaves the area. Young gorillas will sometimes beat their chests while playing.

Communication

Face Expressions

How do mountain gorillas communicate with each other, other wildlife, and people?

Mountain gorillas often communicate without making a sound. Playful gorillas have open mouths, show no teeth, and have relaxed eyes. Scared gorillas' eyes will dart around, and their mouths will be open to show their teeth. Gorillas who feel threatened or aggressive will have a piercing fixed stare with their lips pressed together. Don't stare at a gorilla! They see it as a threat.

Communication G-21

Odors & Smells

How do mountain gorillas communicate with each other, other wildlife, and people?

Mountain gorillas can communicate with each other by chemical odors. These odors could tell other gorillas the animal's identity, age, or sex. Silverbacks seem to be able to change the intensity of their odor. A stronger odor lets intruders know he is there and to stay away.

Communication

Charges & Bluffs

How do mountain gorillas communicate with each other, other wildlife, and people?

Mountain gorillas are fiercely protective of their family. If the silverback leader cannot move his group away from a threat (e.g., people), he might charge. These are usually bluff charges to scare the intruder away. Charges toward people are more likely if the silverback does not hear you coming, or if you encounter a lone silverback or an unhabituated gorilla group. Human injuries from mountain gorillas are very rare.

Charges and bluffs can also happen when two silverbacks are competing to be the leader of a family group.

Group Roles

What are the different roles for members of a mountain gorilla group?

G-23 Family Groups
G-24 Dominant Silverback Male
G-25 Blackback Males
G-26 Additional Silverbacks
G-27 Adult Females
G-28 Pregnant Females
G-29 Dads
G-30 Moms
G-31 Babies
G-32 Juveniles and Teenagers
G-33 Lone Gorillas

Group Roles G-23

Family Groups

What are the different roles for members of a mountain gorilla group?

Mountain gorillas commonly live in family groups. Groups typically have 5-10 members, but some have as few as 2 or as many as 50 individuals. Living in groups means gorillas share responsibilities like parenting and keeping the group safe. Most groups have one silverback, one or more blackback males, several females, and their young. Larger groups can have several silverbacks. In this case the older and more experienced silverback is in charge, is almost always with the younger and less experienced ones following his leadership.

Group Roles G-24

Dominant Silverback Male

What are the different roles for members of a mountain gorilla group?

A silverback mountain gorilla is a sexually mature adult male who can become the leader of the gorilla family group. The black fur on his back begins turning silver at 12-13 years, with the change being complete by 15. The silverback gorilla is the protector of his family, often seen sitting by himself watching and listening for signs of danger. He keeps track of all family members to make sure they are safe and staying close.

We Are Inseparable *Photo: Nick Penny / CTPH*

Group Roles

G-25

Blackback Males

What are the different roles for members of a mountain gorilla group?

An 8 to 12 year old male mountain gorilla is called a blackback. He is a young adult who is not yet sexually mature. The blackback's head is a round shape like all the other gorillas except the silverback. Between 12 to 15 years the black fur on the male's back grows in as silver, signifying his sexual maturity and change of status to a silverback.

Group Roles G-26

Additional Silverbacks

What are the different roles for members of a mountain gorilla group?

When a blackback mountain gorilla becomes sexually mature and his back fur changes to silver, the group's silverback leader will either force him to leave the group or allow him to stay. A few large groups have had two related silverback leaders, with one holding the clear dominant role. if the second silverback grows bigger and stronger, he might try to forcefully take over as leader or he might leave the group to attract other females and begin his own family.

We Are Inseparable *Photo: Naboth Akampurira*

Group Roles

Adult Females

What are the different roles for members of a mountain gorilla group?

A mountain gorilla group can have one, a few, or many adult females. The older females are leaders to the younger ones. The females are mothers and aunties, spending much of their time caring for the young gorillas. When a female becomes sexually mature, she will leave the group of her birth to join another group and mate with a silverback outside of her family. Although she chooses the silverback she wants, the females of that group decide whether to accept her into their group or not.

Group Roles G-28

Pregnant Females

What are the different roles for members of a mountain gorilla group?

Females start mating between 7 and 8 years, and have their first babies around 10. Pregnancy lasts 8.5 months, just a little shorter than humans. A female gorilla normally has one baby every 4-5 years. Twins are very rare.

Group Roles

Dads

G-29

What are the different roles for members of a mountain gorilla group?

For many years scientists thought the dominant silverback leader was the only father of the young in the group. DNA evidence now confirms that some females allow other silverbacks in the group to mate with them secretly. Mating happens only when a female is in heat.

Group Roles

Moms

What are the different roles for members of a mountain gorilla group?

A mountain gorilla mother is loving, gentle, and protective. She does not allow other gorillas to touch the baby during birth or to care for the newborn. For the first three years of life, babies sleep with their mother. By the age of four the young gorilla is independent enough to stop nursing and feed entirely on solid food. Once this happens, the mother is able to get pregnant again.

Group Roles

Babies

What are the different roles for members of a mountain gorilla group?

Baby mountain gorillas are dependent upon their mothers during the first three years of life. For the first few months they stay in mother's arms. At about six months babies start riding on their mother's back. By nine months the young ones are eating fresh leaves, playing with other babies, and beginning to explore close to mom. Once babies are a year old, the mom allows them to play farther away while she and other family members keep a careful watch.

Group Roles G-32

Juveniles and Teenagers

What are the different roles for members of a mountain gorilla group?

Mountain gorillas are called juveniles between ages 3-6, and teenagers or subadults between ages 6-8. These youngsters are treated with affection and incredible patience. They spend their days playing, climbing, and exploring. The mothers and aunties make sure they do not wander too far. Discipline for unwanted behavior can be a grunt, a stern look, or an irritated posture.

Group Roles G-33

Lone Gorillas

What are the different roles for members of a mountain gorilla group?

Some adult male mountain gorillas live alone. A young silverback who has left his birth family often lives alone until he can attract females from other groups to join him.

3

Ecosystems of Bwindi Impenetrable Forest

Forest Ecosystems

Animals of the forest

Plants of the forest

Forest Ecosystems

How do parts of the forest interact as a balanced ecosystem?

- F-1   Land of Mist
- F-2   Mountain Rainforest
- F-3   Sunny Meadows
- F-4   Thick Undergrowth
- F-5   Forest Soil
- F-6   Forest Water Catchment
- F-7   Groundwater to Wells
- F-8   Forest Streams

Forest Ecosystems F-1

Land of Mist

How do parts of the forest interact as a balanced ecosystem?

This ancient rainforest has an average yearly rainfall of 140-190 cm (54-58 inches). It has many different types of trees, bushes, flowers, and grasses that create homes and provide food for the animals. The plants also act like a net to catch and hold the moisture from the rains. This often creates a mist that covers the mountains.

Forest Ecosystems

Mountain Rainforest

How do parts of the forest interact as a balanced ecosystem?

The varying altitudes of these mountains create diverse environments for different species of plants to grow. The forest has over 400 indigenous plant species that live in sunny and shady areas, warmer low altitudes and cooler high altitudes, and wet and dry soils.

Forest Ecosystems F-3

Sunny Meadows

How do parts of the forest interact as a balanced ecosystem?

The rainforest also has grassy open meadows. Antelope and other animals visit these areas to feed plants that thrive in the full sun. Mountain gorillas and elephants help create sunny areas in the forests when they pull up larger plants to eat.

Forest Ecosystems F-4

Thick Undergrowth

How do parts of the forest interact as a balanced ecosystem?

Many plants grow under and around the larger trees of this mountain rainforest, creating shade throughout the day and making it hard to walk through. In some places the plants are so thick that people need to use pangas to cut a path. The descriptive name of Bwindi Impenetrable Forest fits! The dense plant growth helps keep the soil moist and water in the streams, and in turn provide food and shelter for animals.

Forest Ecosystems F-5

Forest Soil

How do parts of the forest interact as a balanced ecosystem?

The dense forest plant life helps keep water in the forest's soil, streams, and groundwater. The roots of plants hold the nutrient-rich soil in place and prevent erosion. When the plants die, they decompose (break down) and add nutrients back into the soil. When it rains, the water is held in the layers of plants or soaks into the sponge-like soil. Some water flows into streams and other water moves deep underground, becoming groundwater. The plant-covered soil helps slow the flow of water down the mountains and into the farmland and villages.

Forest Ecosystems F-6

Forest Water Catchment

How do parts of the forest interact as a balanced ecosystem?

The forest is the water catchment basin (watershed) that provides water to surrounding villages. When rains fall in the forest, water can stay on the surface, making its way into streams and eventually out of the forest. It can also soak into the spongy forest soils to collect as groundwater. Village wells can pump this groundwater back to the surface for people to use. As long as the forest is healthy, this water catchment can continue to provide a reliable source of stream water and groundwater.

Forest Ecosystems

Groundwater to Wells

How do parts of the forest interact as a balanced ecosystem?

Rain in the mountain rainforest soaks deep into the spongy soil to add to the groundwater. Unlike surface water in streams or lakes, groundwater is found underground in the spaces between soils, pebbles, and rocks. It can be pumped back to the surface by a well. A healthy forest means more groundwater is captured from rains, and more water is available from wells.

Forest Ecosystems

F-8

Forest Streams

How do parts of the forest interact as a balanced ecosystem?

Rain that falls in the mountain rainforest often collects in the many forest streams. Dense plant life slows the flow of stream water down the mountain and out of the forest, helping prevent floods and keep water in the streams during the dry season. After reaching villages, this water is used for drinking, cooking, farming, herding, and more.

Animals of the Forest

How do the native animals affect the Bwindi forest ecosystem?

- F-9 Gorillas (Engagi)
- F-10 Chimpanzee (Empundu)
- F-11 Forest Elephant (Enjojo)
- F-12 Duikers (Efumbiri)
- F-13 Baboons (Enkobe)
- F-14 Colobus monkey (Enkyende)
- F-15 Golden monkey (Enkyende)
- F-16 Red-tailed monkey (Enkyende)
- F-17 L'Hoest's monkey (Enkyende)
- F-18 Bush pig (Empunu)
- F-19 Pangolin (Engamba)
- F-20 Bees (Enjokyi)
- F-21 Butterflies (Ekyihuguhugu)
- F-22 Birds (Enyonyi)

Animals of the Forest F-9

Gorillas (Engagi)

How do the native animals affect the Bwindi forest ecosystem?

Mountain gorillas live in family groups that slowly eat their way through the forest in search of their favorite foods. They are called ecosystem engineers because they change which plants grow where. When they pull up plants to eat, they break up the soil so new plants have space to grow. Seeds are spread to new places when gorillas groom each other and toss down any seeds that were stuck in fur. After eating fruits, they drop seeds on the ground, or the seeds pass through their digestive system and reach the soil in their feces. Gorilla poo also fertilizes the soil.

Animals of the Forest   F-10

Chimpanzees (Empundu)

How do the native animals affect the Bwindi forest ecosystem?

Gorillas aren't the only great ape in Bwindi – chimpanzees live in the forest as well. Like their close relatives, chimps live in large family groups and spend time on the ground and in trees. They eat mostly plants and fruits and will occasionally eat smaller animals. They are very intelligent and curious mammals.

We Are Inseparable   Photo: Erik Arndt

Animals of the Forest

Forest Elephants (Enjojo)

How do the native animals affect the Bwindi forest ecosystem?

Bwindi is home to a small number of elephants who have adapted to the forest. They are called ecosystem engineers because their behavior changes the environment around them. As they walk through the forest, they trample plants, eat them, and pull them up. This opens space for new plants to grow that create food and shelter for other wildlife.

Animals of the Forest

Duikers (Efumbiri)

How do the native animals affect the Bwindi forest ecosystem?

The black-fronted duikers and yellow-back duikers are small, shy forest antelope. They eat plants and stay hidden in the thick brush. At dawn and dusk these animals sometimes move into open meadows to feed. Duikers are sometimes killed illegally by people in need of protein to help their families survive. During the 80,000 years the Batwa lived in the forest, the duiker was one of a variety of animals they sustainably hunted for food.

Animals of the Forest

F-13

Baboons (Enkobe)

How do the native animals affect the Bwindi forest ecosystem?

Baboons eat anything and go anywhere. They live on the ground and will eat leaves, berries, flowers, seeds, roots, bark sap, fish, spiders, worms, smaller monkeys, rodents, and more. Because they are not picky eaters, these monkeys can live in places where others cannot. They're often seen on the edges of the forest and around villages. People are watchful for baboons because they can be aggressive, destroy crops, and cause other problems. Baboons live in troops (groups) of 5-250 individuals.

Animals of the Forest　　　　　　　　　　　　　　　　　　F-14

Colobus Monkey (Enkyende)

How do the native animals affect the Bwindi forest ecosystem?

These leaf-eaters spend almost all of their lives in the treetops. They live in troops (groups) of 5-10 individuals. When they leap from branch to branch, their long white cape of hair and tails slow their fall. This monkey was given the name colobus because it does not have thumbs like other monkeys – "Colobus" means "mutilated" in Greek.

Animals of the Forest F-15

Golden Monkey (Enkyende)

How do the native animals affect the Bwindi forest ecosystem?

The golden monkey spends most of its time at lower altitudes in the bamboo forest. It is much smaller than a gorilla and has a long tail, staying in the trees much of the day.

Animals of the Forest — F-16

Red-Tailed Monkey (Enkyende)

How do the native animals affect the Bwindi forest ecosystem?

These fruit-eating monkeys spend their time in trees. They have white noses and cheeks, and a long red tail. They pack their large cheek pouches with fruit, leaves, flowers, or insects and then move away from others in the group to eat. These monkeys live in groups of 20-30 individuals and are active during the day.

Animals of the Forest F-17

L'Hoest's Monkey (Enkyende)

How do the native animals affect the Bwindi forest ecosystem?

These large monkeys are recognized by their large beard of white fur. They spend most of their time on the ground, running up into trees if threatened. They eat many parts of plants as well as worms, spiders, grasshoppers, ants, and other insects. Males are larger than females and have a bright blue scrotum (testicles). The brighter the color, the more attractive the male can be to females.

Animals of the Forest F-18

Bush Pig (Empunu)

How do the native animals affect the Bwindi forest ecosystem?

These tusked animals are diggers. They are very dangerous when they feel threatened or are surprised. Bush pigs eat plant roots, tubers (underground stems), and other buried plant parts. They also eat fruits and insect larvae next to the ground. They are good swimmers and will wade into water to find plants to eat. Bushpigs will live near the edge of the forest close to villages and might come into farm fields in search of food.

When the Indigenous Batwa lived in the forest, they sustainably hunted the bush pig for food.

Animals of the Forest

Pangolin (Engamba)

How do the native animals affect the Bwindi forest ecosystem?

The Bwindi forest is home to the endangered white-bellied pangolin, also called the tree pangolin. These animals are slow-moving and mostly active at night. Pangolins, nicknamed the scaly anteaters, catch and eat ants and termites with their sticky tongues. They climb trees, using their prehensile tails to grasp and hang from branches. Their bodies are covered by large scales. When threatened or startled. they roll in a ball so only their sharp scale armor is exposed. The name "pangolin" comes from the Malay word *pengguling*, which means "something that rolls up."

Pangolins are the most trafficked mammal in the world. National and international laws make it illegal to harm or kill these endangered animals. They are killed for meat; for traditional medicines from claws and scales; for boots and bags from the leathery skin; and jewelry from the scales. Pangolin Rescue Center in Kanungu rescues and cares for pangolins who wander out of the national park, and returns the animals to the forest when healthy. https://www.facebook.com/pangolinrescuecenter

Animals of the Forest *F-20*

Bees (Enjokyi)

How do the native animals affect the Bwindi forest ecosystem?

Five species of stingless bees are indigenous to Bwindi. They are essential pollinators to help many of the forest's flowering plants produce seeds for the next generation. Wild honey is a favorite food and medicine of the BATWA and other people living around the forest. People build apiaries to encourage bees to build hives outside of the forest so honey can still be collected and enjoyed as food. A concern is that bees are dying from chemicals in pesticides and herbicides, from changes in their forest habitat, and from invasive species.

Animals of the Forest F-21

Butterflies (Ekyihuguhugu)

How do the native animals affect the Bwindi forest ecosystem?

Over 300 butterfly species call Bwindi home. They help pollinate plants when they travel from flower to flower to drink the sweet nectar. People travel from around the world to see the butterflies of Bwindi.

Animals of the Forest F-22

Birds (Enyonyi)

How do the native animals affect the Bwindi forest ecosystem?

Bwindi has 346 species of birds, 23 of which are endemic to this ancient forest – they are found nowhere else in the world! Many birds are seed eaters who help move seeds from one place to another in the forest. Some drink nectar and pollinate flowers. Others catch and eat other animals or eat animals that have died. Some commonly seen birds are the great blue turaco, Rossi's turaco, black and white casqued hornbill, Newmann's warbler, Shelly's crimson wing, African green broadbill, Grauer's rush warbler, and Chapin's flycatcher "Muscicapa lendu." Birdwatchers from around the world come to see Bwindi's birds.

Plants of the Forest

What are some native forest plants and how do they help the ecosystem and people?

F-23   Mahogany Tree (Omuyovii)
F-24   Ficus Tree (Ekyitoma)
F-25   Ceiba Tree (Ekitoma)
F-26   Africa Tree Fern (Ekigunju)
F-27   Edible and Medicinal Plants
F-28   Favorite Plants of People
F-29   Food for Wildlife
F-30   Favorite Foods of Gorillas

Plants of the Forest — F-23

Mahogany Tree (Omuyovii)

What are some native forest plants and how do they help the ecosystem and people?

The African brown mahogany is one of the taller trees in Bwindi, towering over others at 65 meters (312 feet). It is illegal to cut this tree in Bwindi, but it is a target for loggers in unprotected areas. The tree's very straight trunk and beautiful wood make it valuable to cut and sell to be made into furniture and other wood products around the world.

Plants of the Forest F-24

Ficus Trees (Ekyitoma)

What are some native forest plants and how do they help the ecosystem and people?

The Ficus tree is one of the biggest trees in Bwindi, reaching heights of around 90 meters. It can grow up and around other trees, eventually fully enclosing and strangling them. The base of the tree can have large roots above the ground called buttresses. Traditional Batwa clothing and shelter are made from Ficus bark. It is one of the oldest textiles.

Plants of the Forest

Ceiba Tree (Ekitoma)

What are some native forest plants and how do they help the ecosystem and people?

This tree species is one of the tallest in Bwindi (70 meters, 230 feet) and can be seen poking high above oother trees making up the forest canopy. It can live over 500 years. It has enormous roots that begin above ground and expand out from the trunk in buttresses. Some roots attach to the trunk as high as 3 meters above the ground, helping to keep the tree from tipping over. Ceiba trees create homes for many animals and are protected from loggers in BINP. Ceiba bark has been used by the Indigenous Batwa to make traditional clothing and shelter. This is one of the oldest textiles.

Plants of the Forest — F-26

African Tree Fern (Ekigunju)

What are some native forest plants and how do they help the ecosystem and people?

The tree fern is seen throughout the forest. Indigenous Batwa can determine the age of these trees by the number of stems forming the trunk. Some parts of the fern tree are used for weaving baskets and other items. Fern shoots (stems) can be eaten. When the Batwa lived in the forest they used the rough stem as a hair comb and the large leaves to make soft beds for the elders.

Plants of the Forest

F-27

Edible & Medicinal Plants

What are some native forest plants and how do they help the ecosystem and people?

Bwindi is a pharmacy and supermarket of medicinal and edible plants, many of which are found nowhere else in the world. The wide variety of fruits are favorites for both people and wildlife. Other plants can treat health issues ranging from simple cuts and allergies to back pain, ulcers, and life-threatening illnesses. The Batwa, who lived in harmony with the forest plants and animals until 1991, have 80,000 years of traditional knowledge about the edible and medicinal uses of forest plants. Today, gathering these plants by local residents is only allowed in controlled multi-use areas of the park, or outside park boundaries.

Plants of the Forest

F-28

Favorite Plants of People

**Ekyerere
(African basil, Ocimum)**

**Encerere
(Wild Berries, Rubus pinnatus)**

**Entodwere
(Impatiens)**

**Ekifenesi
(Jackfruit)**

Bwindi has many edible fruits, leaves, stems, and roots. Here are a few popular forest plants that are now grown outside of the forest around homes.

We Are Inseparable

Photo: Ezera Mugyenyi

Plants of the Forest

F-29

Food for Wildlife

What are some native forest plants and how do they help the ecosystem and people?

The great variety of edible forest plants provide food for plant-eating animals. The mountain gorillas of Bwindi eat the parts of as many as 45 different plants. Depending on the season and location in the forest, gorillas will eat the leaves, stems, and fruits of different plants. In the dry season they might also eat seeds and bark.

Plants of the Forest F-30

Favorite Foods of Gorillas

**Ekitondwere
(Tristemma mauritianum)**

**Omumbya
(Stinging nettle)**

**Ekyunga
("Gorilla sugar cane")**

**Ekyufe
(Myrianthus holstii)**

Here are a few of the 142 different plant species that mountain gorillas are known to eat. Most of their diet is leaves, shoots and stems. Fruits are a favorite treat in Bwindi. Gorillas also eat roots and flowers.

4

Jobs supporting the forest and wildlife

What village jobs help the people, community, forest, and wildlife?

- J-1   Park and UWA Staff
- J-2   Ranger Patrols
- J-3   Ranger Guides & Trackers
- J-4   Gorilla Guardians
- J-5   Wildlife Vets & Scientists
- J-6   Porters for Tourists
- J-7   Drivers for Tourists
- J-8   Lodging and Service Staff
- J-9   Artists and Handcrafters
- J-10 Coffee Farmers
- J-11 Conservation Organization Staff

Jobs supporting the forest and wildlife J-1

Park & UWA Staff

What village jobs help the people, community, forest, and wildlife?

Local residents have the opportunity to help care for something that the rest of the world does not have – this ancient mountain rainforest and the mountain gorillas. Uganda Wildlife Authority (UWA) is responsible for managing the park and wildlife in the Bwindi and Mgahinga Conservation Area (BMCA). The staff patrol the park, monitor wildlife, prevent poaching, engage local communities in conservation, help communities resolve human-wildlife conflicts, and assist with tourism. BINP administrative staff manage the park projects and staff, and are the people who interact with tourists, answer their questions, and prepare them to have a positive experience in the park. They also keep the park running smoothly.

Jobs supporting the forest and wildlife J-2

Ranger Patrols

What village jobs help the people, community, forest, and wildlife?

Ugandans, with many opportunities for local residents, are hired and trained to become rangers by Uganda Wildlife Authority (UWA) to protect the forest, mountain gorillas, and other wildlife. Rangers have many important parts of their job. They are gorilla trackers who make daily trips into the forest to check on the gorilla groups' location, activities, and health. They act as law enforcement in the park, doing anti-poaching patrols to remove snares set illegally to catch animals for bush meat and trade. They watch for other illegal activities like cutting down trees for fuel or construction, or polluting streams.

Jobs supporting the forest and wildlife J-3

Ranger Guides & Trackers

What village jobs help the people, community, forest, and wildlife?

Tourists can get permits to hike into the forest with a ranger to visit a gorilla group. Rangers share their knowledge of the forest and gorillas with the tourists and enforce strict rules and regulations to keep people and gorillas safe during the one-hour visit. Everyone must put on face masks and sanitize their boots before getting near the gorillas. When near a group, rangers make sure tourists stay the designated 10 meters distance away from the gorillas to avoid passing germs to our close relatives. Guides can also lead tourists on forest walks to see other animals and sites of interest. Trackers follow the gorillas every day and notify the guides of their location.

We Are Inseparable *Photo: Laura Arndt, Jeff Sanders*

Jobs supporting the forest and wildlife J-4

Gorilla Guardians

What village jobs help the people, community, forest, and wildlife?

About 140 community residents around Bwindi volunteer as Human and Gorilla Conflict Resolution Teams (HUGOs, aka Gorilla Guardians) with Uganda Wildlife Authority (UWA), Conservation Through Public Health, and other partners in conservation. They are trained by UWA and partners to safely herd gorillas and other wildlife back into the protected forest when the animals wander into peoples' fields and gardens. This reduces conflict between the people and wildlife. Gorilla Guardians also help to monitor gorilla and community health, knowing that the health of one is deeply connected to the health of the other. One way they do this is collecting gorilla fecal samples and monitoring the signs and symptoms of ill health in mountain gorillas and other wildlife.

Jobs supporting the forest and wildlife J-5

Wildlife Vets & Scientists

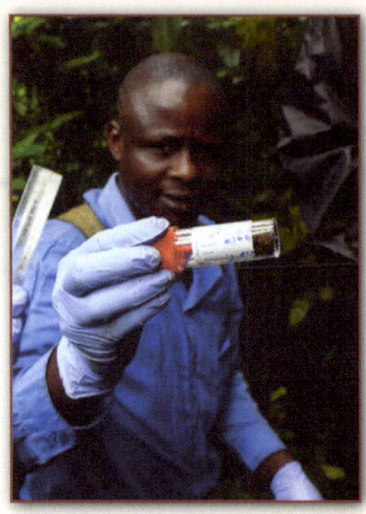
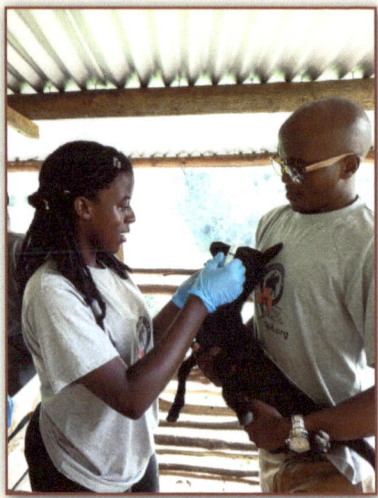

What village jobs help the people, community, forest, and wildlife?

Local and Uganda Wildlife Authority (UWA) veterinarians collaborate to monitor the health of mountain gorillas, livestock, and other wildlife. If a gorilla or another animal gets sick, is injured, or has a life-threatening illness, the veterinarians give medical care. When a gorilla dies, UWA veterinarians work with partner NGO vets to conduct a necropsy (study of the body) to learn more about the animal and the cause of death.

Ugandan scientists and university students conduct research to learn more about the forest, the gorillas, and the people. This research helps BINP, UWA, and villages decide how to care for the land and helps the park develop an effective tourist program.

Jobs supporting the forest and wildlife J-6

Porters for Tourists

What village jobs help the people, community, forest, and wildlife?

Tourists, scientists, and others visiting or working in the forest are encouraged to hire porters to carry their supplies, equipment, and luggage. This job is such an important source of income for local residents and families that a cooperative association was formed to increase equitable opportunities for more porters to be consistently hired and earn an income.

Jobs supporting the forest and wildlife J-7

Drivers for Tourists

What village jobs help the people, community, forest, and wildlife?

Many tourists who travel to the Bwindi area and stay in lodges near the national park need transportation to get around the communities and to the park entrance. Local drivers with cars can offer these driving services.

Jobs supporting the forest and wildlife J-8

Lodging & Service Staff

What village jobs help the people, community, forest, and wildlife?

When tourists visit BINP they stay in lodges and camps, eat at restaurants, and visit shops. These businesses employ many local people to provide services for tourists.

Jobs supporting the forest and wildlife

Artists & Handcrafters

Kaplan Gadson Musinguzi

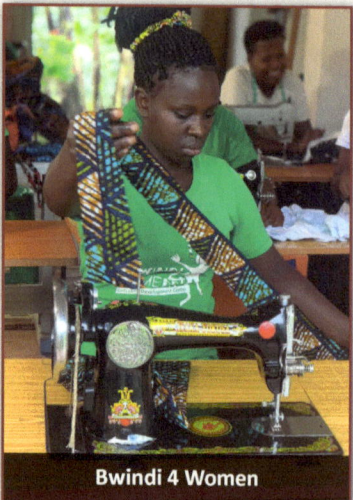

Bwindi 4 Women

What village jobs help the people, community, forest, and wildlife?

Tourists often want to take home a souvenir to remember their time in BINP, or they might want an item that is immediately helpful during their stay. Carvings, toys, musical instruments, weavings, dolls, artwork, fabric, jewelry, and walking sticks are just a few examples. There are so many creative and innovative ways to share culture and environment through art, and to provide items that tourists might need. These are sold in shops and near park entrances.

Jobs supporting the forest and wildlife J-10

Coffee Farmers

What village jobs help the people, community, forest, and wildlife?

Growing coffee is an important source of income for many people around Bwindi, reducing the need to poach and gather resources from the park. One brand, Gorilla Conservation Coffee, has trained over 500 people in sustainable agriculture and business practices to grow and harvest coffee. Sales from this top-rated coffee provide financial stability for individual growers and their families, and support the broader community.

Jobs supporting the forest and wildlife J-11

Conservation Org. Staff

What village jobs help the people, community, forest, and wildlife?

I was convinced that you couldn't keep the gorillas healthy without improving the health and well-being of the people with whom they shared their fragile habitats. My approach to conservation had changed. I started to think of setting up an NGO [now Conservation Through Public Health] that improved the health of wildlife and people together.

Dr. Gladys Kalema-Zikousa, *Walking with Gorillas* (109)

Many nonprofit organizations work around Bwindi to help people and communities, and to protect the forest, mountain gorillas, and other wildlife. The organization, Conservation Through Public Health, focuses on the interconnected health and conservation issues of gorillas, the forest, livestock, and local people.

5

STEAM Conservation Projects

What STEAM* conservation projects can be done in villages to solve problems and sustainably help the people, community, forest, and wildlife?

- P-1   Reduce human-wildlife conflict
- P-2   Reduce community litter
- P-3   Repurpose plastic waste
- P-4   Reforest with native trees
- P-5   Grow edible or medicinal plants
- P-6   Create alternatives for wood fuel
- P-7   Improve hygiene and sanitation
- P-8   Capture rainwater
- P-9   Clean polluted water
- P-10 Provide a reliable source of protein
- P-11 Educate with art or app
- P-12 Build bee apiaries

These STEAM conservation projects are being done by Bwindi Youth Guardian groups, local organizations, and individuals in communities around the national park. If you live near Bwindi, you can get ideas of projects you might like to do in your community. If you don't live around the park, you might read about a local project you'd like to support, or find a project you would like to do in your own community.

To do a STEAM Conservation Project:

1. Choose and investigate a local problem or need that affects your community and people as well as the wildlife and natural place like the forest.
2. Design and do a project that uses STEAM (science, technology, engineering, art, and math) to help solve the problem or meet the need.
3. Share your project, what you have done and learned, and hwo the project has helped the people, community, forest, and wildlife. You could inspire others to help or begin their own conservation projects.

STEAM Conservation Projects P-1

Reduce Human-Wildlife Conflict

Identify and investigate a *problem* that is harmful to people, community, forest, and wildlife.

The Problem: Gorillas, forest elephants, and other wildlife come out of BINP into farmland and villages looking for food. When this happens, crops can be damaged, and both people and animals risk getting injured or killed. For example, gorillas occasionally leave the forest to eat banana skins or eucalyptus tree bark, and people may gather to watch them up close. If they get too close, gorillas can feel threatened and might react with roars or bluff charges to protect themselves and their family. This can frighten the people watching and cause them to react in response.

Design and do a *project* to sustainably solve the problem using STEAM (Science, Technology, Engineering, Art. Math).

STEAM Conservation Project: Design a way to discourage wildlife from raiding crops or going into populated areas so there is less chance of harm to people, animals, and plants.

STEAM Conservation Projects

Reduce Community Litter

Buhoma Community Primary School

Rafiki Football Club

Identify and investigate a ***problem*** that is harmful to people, community, forest, and wildlife.

The Problem: Many villages around BINP lack a complete waste management system, leading to litter on the ground and in the water. Plastic rubbish takes 20-500 years to decompose and collects in rivers and pollutes the local water supply. Bacteria and other harmful germs can grow on all types of litter (even biodegradable), harming people and animals. Gorillas and other wildlife can be curious and investigate litter, and scientists have found gorillas with scabies, measles, and respiratory viruses after coming in close contact with it.

Design and do a ***project*** to sustainably solve the problem using STEAM (Science, Technology, Engineering, Art. Math).

STEAM Conservation Project: Design a plastic and biodegradable waste collection system; teach others to use the system to change community waste disposal behavior and increase understanding of harm from plastic litter.

STEAM Conservation Projects P-3

Repurpose Plastic Waste

Buhoma Community Primary School

Identify and investigate a ***problem*** that is harmful to people, community, forest, and wildlife.

The Problem: Plastic litter is very common around Bwindi. For decades, burying and burning have been the only waste management strategies easily available, both of which harm the health of people, animals, and the forest ecosystem. Burning plastic releases toxic gasses that are harmful to breathe; buried plastic takes up to 200 years to break down and creates 'microplastic' particles that stay in soil and water for many more years. New technologies and strategies are being invented and shared around the world to repurpose plastic waste into useful products.

Design and do a ***project*** to sustainably solve the problem using STEAM (Science, Technology, Engineering, Art. Math).

STEAM Conservation Project: Develop ways to recycle or repurpose plastic waste into useful products. Develop products that reduce the use of plastics.

STEAM Conservation Projects P-4

Reforest with Indigenous Trees

Pangolin Rescue Center

Katembe Primary School

Identify and investigate a *problem* that is harmful to people, community, forest, and wildlife.

The Problem: Most indigenous trees have disappeared outside of BINP, leading to soil erosion, desertification, poor water quality, lower crop yield, and loss of natural ecosystems. Fast-growing forests of eucalyptus trees are common outside the park, providing a source of wood for construction, cooking, and heating. However, these single-species forests lack indigenous plant biodiversity and limit habitat for indigenous animal species to live. Currently, many community projects focus on planting individual trees. These efforts could be even more impactful if trees are planted as diverse community forests (i.e., mini-forests) to encourage the return of indigenous animals and a balanced ecosystem.

Design and do a *project* to sustainably solve the problem using STEAM (Science, Technology, Engineering, Art. Math).

STEAM Conservation Project: Plant community forests of indigenous trees to reduce impacts of deforestation and climate change, and to provide resources.

STEAM Conservation Projects

Grow Edible & Medicinal Plants

Action for Minority Children

Action for Minority Children

Identify and investigate a ***problem*** that is harmful to people, community, forest, and wildlife.

The Problem: Many people lack access to indigenous edible and medicinal plants because they are only found within BINP. It is illegal to collect plants within BINP except for in designated areas supervised by park rangers. If planted outside of the forest, these indigenous species could increase the availability of healthy foods and traditional medicines for people in need of an alternative to community health care services. The benefits of some forest plants are threatened by illegal gathering and by the loss of traditional Batwa knowledge as time passes.

Design and do a ***project*** to sustainably solve the problem using STEAM (Science, Technology, Engineering, Art. Math).

STEAM Conservation Project: Grow, harvest, share, and/or educate others about edible or medicinal indigenous plants to reduce the need to go into BINP to collect them and to expand understanding and access to these plants.

STEAM Conservation Projects   P-6

Create Alternatives for Wood Fuel

Identify and investigate a ***problem*** that is harmful to people, community, forest, and wildlife.

The Problem: People need a reliable and healthy source of energy for cooking, heating, lighting, and to run factories. Electricity is unreliable and unavailable in some areas, so wood is used instead. Breathing smoke from wood fires can be harmful to peoples' health and well-being. Burning wood also releases greenhouse gasses (carbon dioxide) that increase the impacts of climate change, such as hotter temperatures or more intense wet and dry periods around BINP. There are few affordable and reliable renewable or low-carbon energy products options to replace wood as an energy source.

Design and do a ***project*** to sustainably solve the problem using STEAM (Science, Technology, Engineering, Art. Math).

STEAM Conservation Project: Develop or use a low-carbon or renewable energy technology for electricity, cooking, lighting, or heating to reduce cutting trees and improve people's health.

We Are Inseparable   *Photos: Jamestgurley, C-Quest Capital*

STEAM Conservation Projects P-7

Improve Hygiene & Sanitation

Identify and investigate a ***problem*** that is harmful to people, community, forest, and wildlife.

The Problem: Lack of available toilets, hand washing stations, and sanitation infrastructure can allow the spread of infectious diseases between people, livestock, and wildlife. People can unintentionally pass diseases to gorillas and wildlife when the animals come out of the forest into areas where people live.

Design and do a ***project*** to sustainably solve the problem using STEAM (Science, Technology, Engineering, Art. Math).

STEAM Conservation Project: Improve availability and use of hygiene and sanitation services to reduce the spread of germs between people, livestock, gorillas, and other wildlife.

STEAM Conservation Projects   P-8

Capture Rainwater

Action for Minority Children

Identify and investigate a ***problem*** that is harmful to people, community, forest, and wildlife.

The Problem: Many residents around BINP do not have easy and reliable access to clean water. The villages near the forest can receive 1,400-1,900 mm (55-75 in) of rain in a year, with most falling during March-April and September-November. Most of this water runs off roofs into the ground instead of being captured and stored for later use.

Design and do a ***project*** to sustainably solve the problem using STEAM (Science, Technology, Engineering, Art. Math).

STEAM Conservation Project: Design a way to collect and store rainwater to use as a source of clean water.

We Are Inseparable   *Photo: Laura Arndt*

STEAM Conservation Projects   P-9

Clean Polluted Water

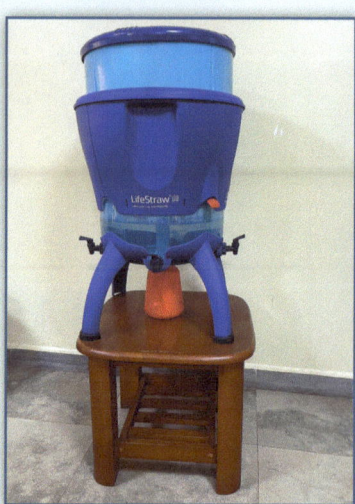

Identify and investigate a *problem* that is harmful to people, community, forest, and wildlife.

The Problem: Reliable clean water is not available for many people. Some people get drinking water from rivers or other water sources that are also used by livestock and wildlife. This can be a source of disease transmission between people, gorillas, and other wildlife. In addition, rubbish of all kinds ends up in or around water sources, polluting the water and leading to health issues. In addition to typical litter, pollution can also include tiny pieces of plastic called microplastics that can build up over time and harm people and animals.

Design and do a *project* to sustainably solve the problem using STEAM (Science, Technology, Engineering, Art. Math).

STEAM Conservation Project: Design a way to clean water after it is collected so it safe to drink. Or design a way to reduce soil erosion and contamination from chemicals or solid waste into the water source before collecting it.

STEAM Conservation Projects   P-10

Provide a Reliable Protein Source

St. Mathew's Nursery & Primary School

Gorilla Guardian Youth Group

Identify and investigate a ***problem*** that is harmful to people, community, forest, and wildlife.

The Problem: Some people lack reliable protein sources and go into the forest looking for protein-rich food, especially bush meat. Some set snares to catch duiker and bush pigs to eat or sell. Other animals, including gorillas, can unintentionally get caught in these traps, become permanently injured, and even die. When looking for food in the forest, people can also unintentionally surprise and scare a gorilla group. The silverback's reaction to protect his family can scare people, leading them to harm or kill the gorilla in self-defense. This is what happened to Rafiki, the former lead silverback of the Nkuringo Gorilla Group.

Design and do a ***project*** to sustainably solve the problem using STEAM (Science, Technology, Engineering, Art. Math).

STEAM Conservation Project: Grow or raise a sustainable plant or animal protein source to reduce the need to hunt or collect food in the forest.

STEAM Conservation Projects — P-11

Educate with Art or App

Identify and investigate a ***problem*** that is harmful to people, community, forest, and wildlife.

The Problem: Some people in our community might not know very much about the forest and gorillas, and how their health is directly linked to human health. They might have misconceptions and not understand all the ways that the forest and gorillas benefit us. Some people might not know how or why to take care of our village and forest environment. So how can we get more people in our village to care about the forest and mountain gorillas, to be proud of living next to BINP and the gorillas' home, and know what to do to help people by taking care of the forest and wildlife?

Design and do a ***project*** to sustainably solve the problem using STEAM (Science, Technology, Engineering, Art. Math).

STEAM Conservation Project: Create educational art or a phone app to teach people how to help solve a conservation problem, or how the forest and wildlife of Bwindi are unique and worth protecting.

We Are Inseparable — *Photos: Roy Gilham, Roger Arndt*

STEAM Conservation Projects P-12

Build Bee Apiaries

Identify and investigate a ***problem*** that is harmful to people, community, forest, and wildlife.

The Problem: Bees provide many benefits to people and ecosystems: they make honey, pollinate plants, and can even deter larger animals from an area. Most indigenous bees live in the forest of BINP, but it is illegal to go into the forest to gather honey or wax. Edible and medicinal plants grown in villages, as well as cash crops like coffee and tea, are dependent on flower pollinators like bees but many farms are far from beehives within the forest. In some areas, forest elephants leave the forest to raid crops. Forest elephants do not like bees and will stay away from beehives. For bees to establish hives near villages they need an inviting site for a hive and a reliable flower food source.

Design and do a ***project*** to sustainably solve the problem using STEAM (Science, Technology, Engineering, Art. Math).

STEAM Conservation Project: Build a bee apiary and care for the bees to solve a problem with access to food or medicine, or a wildlife conflict problem.

We Are Inseparable   *Photos: Laura Arndt, József Szabó*

Learn About Bwindi Youth Guardians and STEAM Projects

Stories and photos of Bwindi Youth Guardian STEAM conservation projects and Bwindi Cards
https://bit.ly/BwindiCards

Bwindi Youth Guardians
are called to action to complete
STEAM Conservation Projects around Bwindi

Follow or contact Laura at
Facebook: @GlobalGreenSTEM
LinkedIn: @LauraSandersArndt
Instagram: @global_greenstem
Website: www.globalgreenstem.com

Year 1 STEAM Conservation Projects funded by

When an eBook, paper book, or pdf of Bwindi Cards is purchased, a portion is contributed to a fund for Bwindi Youth Guardian group microgrants that help

- finance STEAM conservation projects
- cover expenses and fees for Bwindi Youth Guardians to go on ranger-guided forest walks and gorilla treks in Bwindi Impenetrable National Park
- buy *We are Inseparable* books or Bwindi Cards for schools around Bwindi

If you're inspired to find out more about supporting a project, or you want to buy a book or Bwindi Cards, just scan the QR code, go to https://bit.ly/4Bwindi, or talk with Laura at lauraarndt@globalgreenstem.com.

BWINDI CARDS STORY

The idea for ***Bwindi Cards: We Are Inseparable*** began taking shape in 1987 when Laura first started developing conservation education programs for Rwandan youth with Dian Fossey's The Digit Fund (original name)  soon after Fossey's murder. There was a clear need for educational materials about the relationship between the forest ecosystem, the mountain gorillas, and the people living nearby.

In 1991 a poster was designed in Kinyarwandan and displayed in Kinigi and Ruhengeri businesses around Rwanda's Volcanoes National Park office. All programs ceased in 1994 at the start of the genocide.

In 2001 programs shifted to Uganda with a different organization. Version 1 Bwindi Cards were reviewed, edited, and approved by Ugandan educators, national park staff, conservation organization staff, and Makerere University students. This version was printed and distributed to schools around Bwindi Impenetrable National Park (BINP).

Bwindi Card workshop participants. Kabale, Uganda, 2001.

Fast forward to 2023. Global GreenSTEM (Laura) and Conservation Through Public Health -CTPH (Dr. Glady Kalema-Zikusoka) launched a program in villages around BINP for Bwindi Youth Guardian groups to design and do STEAM conservation projects that help solve problems affecting people, the forest ecosystem, and mountain gorillas. (Funding from National Geographic Society.)

The *We Are Inseparable - Bwindi Cards* (2024) are being used by the Bwindi Youth Guardians, CTPH, and park rangers.
https://bit.ly/BwindiCards

ABOUT THE AUTHOR

Laura Sanders Arndt is the creator of culturally-relevant purposeful STEM experiences, and the founder of Global GreenSTEM. She works with educators to design solutions-based STEM opportunities and curricula that inspire and empower learners of any culture and identity to be changemakers. A few of Laura's collaborations have been to develop and adapt Pacific-island-based STEM curriculum for Guam schools; co-develop a school's Indigenized STEAM curriculum and projects to amplify the voices of North American Indigenous students; and empower Bwindi Youth Guardians to design and carry out STEAM conservation projects to help solve problems in their communities near Bwindi Impenetrable National Park.

Laura has worked with several international mountain gorilla organizations since 1987 to create conservation education programs and action projects for Rwandan and Ugandan youth. The youth STEAM conservation projects were recently established in partnership with Ugandan-based Conservation Through Public Health. This book version of the Bwindi Cards is a part of that program.

Laura's work is enriched by her sixteen years of experience teaching high school and elementary science and GreenSTEM in Colorado, as well as her numerous collaborations with local, national, and international organizations and agencies. Laura also designs and conducts professional learning for schools, districts, and organizations; speaks at conferences; and writes articles.

Laura's life-long love and respect for the natural world and people of all cultures began as a child growing up with her adventurous nature- and travel-loving family in mid-Missouri (USA). She raised her two children, Erik and Cory, with husband-partner Roger in Colorado surrounded by a ponderosa pine forest on the ancestral homeland of the Ute, Cheyenne and Oceti Sakowin Nations. This is where she continues to live, work, and thrive.

www.ingramcontent.com/pod-product-compliance
Lightning Source LLC
Chambersburg PA
CBHW040934030426
42337CB00001B/5